NUMBER KIT 1

Fewer or greater?

Subtraction and addition

British Library Cataloguing-in-Publication Data
A catalogue record for this book is available from the British Library.

ISBN 0-590-53583-8

Published by Scholastic Ltd
Villiers House
Clarendon Avenue
Leamington Spa
Warwickshire CV32 5PR

© 1996 Scholastic Ltd
123456789 6789012345

AUTHOR
Trisha Henley

SERIES CONSULTANT
Sheila Ebbutt
Director of BEAM (Be A Mathematician) which is supported by Islington Council

CURRICULUM LINKS
Ian Gardner, Maths Curriculum Adviser, (England and Wales), Julie Parkin, with Edinburgh Centre for Mathematics Education (Scotland) and Michael Wallace (Northern Ireland)

The publishers wish to thank the following individuals and organisations for their invaluable help in developing the *Maths Focus* concept: Jayne de Courcy, Courcy Consultants; Dr Daphne Kerslake; West Sussex Maths Centre, West Sussex Institute; Oxfordshire Maths Centre; Edinburgh Centre for Mathematics Education; David Bell, Assistant Director for Education, Newcastle-upon-Tyne; Professor Geoffrey and Dr Julia Matthews

EDITORIAL TEAM
Angela Dewsbury and Jo Saxelby-Jennings

SERIES DESIGNER
Joy White

DESIGNERS
Toby Long

COVER PHOTOGRAPH
© Scholastic Inc.

ILLUSTRATORS
Val Biro, Roma Bishop (John Martin & Artists), Sonia Canals, Debbie Clark (Simon Girling Assoc.), Trevor Dunton, Emma Holt (Sylvie Poggio), Claire James (Graham-Cameron), Lorna Kent, Derek Matthews, Chris Russell, Peter Read, Mick Reid (Peters, Fraser and Dunlop) and The Drawing Room. Postman Pat™ ©Woodland Animations Ltd 1995. Licensed by Copyrights.

POSTERMAT
Martyn Chillmaid; wall built by Daniel Mullaney using LEGO; we acknowledge ©LEGO-Dacta (UK) for their permission.

Designed using Aldus Pagemaker
Processed by PAGES Bureau, Leamington Spa
Printed in Great Britain by Ebenezer Baylis & Son, Worcester and George Over, Rugby

© Material from the National Curriculum, Scottish 5–14 Guidelines and the Northern Ireland Curriculum is Crown copyright and is reproduced by permission of the Controller of HMSO, 1995.

CONTENTS

MATHS FOCUS

Maths Focus can be used to:

▶ **assess children's knowledge and skills;**

▶ **offer reinforcement activities to develop understanding;**

▶ **provide enrichment activities to consolidate and extend the learning;**

▶ **develop skills and ability in using and applying mathematics.**

DIFFERENTIATION

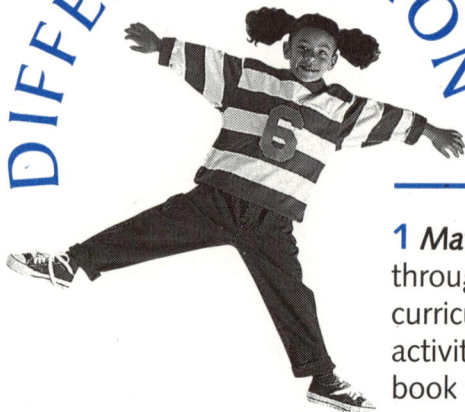

1 *Maths Focus* offers structured progression of content and skills through the Kits 1–5* and provides links with all UK national curricula. With a particular clakss or year group, you may use activities from more than one kit to cater for all ability levels. Each book focuses on a specific mathematical concept, with activities set in a range of contexts – including games, stories, problems, everyday situations and puzzles – so that children learn to use their mathematics flexibly and appropriately.

2 Assessment activities allow you to evaluate the children's ability to use and apply the mathematics they have learned.

3 Understanding is developed through two types of activity:
▶ **Reinforcement activities** – which increase children's confidence by concentrating on specific concept or skill and presenting the maths in a variety of contexts;
▶ **Enrichment activities** – which consolidate and extend children's learning in more open-ended contexts.

4 Extension ideas at the end of each activity offer ways for more able children to go further in their exploration of a concept.

See inside back cover for overview of kits and curriculum coverage.

offers...

USING & APPLYING

Aspects of **Using and Applying** covered by each activity are given in the teacher's notes. To help with your planning, the grid on page 9 and the teachers' notes highlight how problem solving, communication and logical reasoning are built into each activity.

ASSESSMENT

Maths Focus offers two types of assessment to be used when you feel appropriate to plan the best way forward for each child.

▶ You may want to use the **Diagnostic assessment** activity at the start of teaching a concept to establish the existing level of understanding. Alternatively, use it after some initial teaching, to provide a check on progress.

▶ The **Assessment double-check** allows you to assess the child's understanding of the concept as a whole, to see how their learning has progressed.

FLEXIBLE RESOURCE

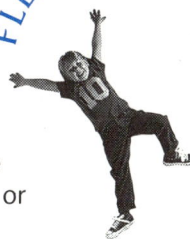

Maths Focus can be used in a variety of ways to support your teaching of mathematics and your style of teaching, allowing you to use the activities with individuals, groups or the whole class.

Use **Maths Focus** activities alongside a published scheme to:
▶ develop children's understanding of specific concepts in a greater range of contexts;
▶ assess children's understanding of a concept, and then to support or extend it with differentiated activities;
▶ focus on the using and applying aspect of the mathematics curriculum.

If you don't use a published scheme use **Maths Focus**:
▶ as a core resource when planning your own scheme of work;
▶ to teach and assess specific concepts.

USING TALK

All teachers' notes pages offer questions you can ask children to encourage them to talk about what they are doing. Use the questions while they are working to focus their mathematical thinking or at the end of the activity to assess their level of understanding. Most pages also offer:
▶ **Here's the maths** – explanations of the maths included in the activity;
▶ **What to look for** – diagnostic pointers to help you to assess whether the child has achieved the mathematical aim of the activity;
▶ **More help needed** – ways to help children are who struggling with the activity.

RANGE OF RESOURCES

Maths Focus kits come with a full-colour laminated postermat for each book. This flexible wipe-clean resource can be used with a number of the activities in its book and also as a general mathematics resource. Each book has a black and white photocopiable version of its postermat, to use with the activities and for permanent recording of the children's work. Extra postermats are available separately (see inside back cover).

The activities in each book are planned to use a range of mathematical resources, including counting apparatus, number lines and grids and calculators. Mental maths is emphasised throughout.

Children need experience of all three aspects of subtraction to grasp the concept early on and see it as one operation. Activities involving addition as well will increase their confidence with both operations.

Here's the maths…
Subtraction and addition

What's involved

▶ Children need to picture in their minds what is happening when they are adding and subtracting to be able to use these operations to solve problems. They need to link the '−' and '+' symbols to particular situations and, over time, to recognise which types of problem can be solved in this way.

▶ The two concepts of addition and subtraction are interrelated: they are inverse or 'opposite' operations. Although the emphasis in this book is on subtraction, addition will naturally come into most of the activities. Children need to understand the relationship between the two operations and, at a later stage, know that if 9 − 7 = 2, then 2 + 7 = 9 and 7 + 2 = 9 but that 7 − 9 does not equal 2. So from the beginning of their mathematical experiences children should be involved with both addition and subtraction. Opportunities to discuss their activities are vital if they are to understand the relationships between the two.

▶ Children often see the three aspects of subtraction – taking away from a set; comparing numbers to find the difference; inverse or complementary addition – as being very different. To help them understand that they are all the one operation, subtraction, they need to experience a variety of situations which provide a balance of the three aspects – too much concentration on 'take away', for example, may lead children to misunderstand the nature of subtraction.

TAKING AWAY FROM A SET

▶ Subtraction allows us to find out in number what remains when something has been taken away. As adults we encounter this type of problem often, for example, when we calculate our bank balance.

▶ For children, these tasks need to be practical at first, and in the form of real situations. For example, if we have a tin of ten pencils and four are taken out, six will be left in the tin. Since the children can 'see' what is happening, they can usually understand this aspect of subtraction fairly easily.

COMPLEMENTARY ADDITION

▶ Inverse or complementary addition is used to find out what must be added to a number, to make a given total; for example, 7 + ? = 10. We use this aspect of subtraction often, for example, when we look at our watches and calculate how long we must wait until the bus is due.

▶ Children often encounter this type of task when, as a shopkeeper in the class shop, they must calculate the amount of change to give.

▶ Again, the tasks should be set in a practical context. For example: 'We had ten pencils in this pot, and now there are seven. How many do we need to find?' The children should keep adding one, until they reach the total. Later they will work using their fingers, and then in their heads.

KEY FACTS

• There are three aspects to subtraction:
• taking away from a set;
• comparing numbers to find the difference;
• inverse or complementary addition (for example: 'What must be added to 7 to make 10?').

COMPARISON OR DIFFERENCE

▶ Subtraction is also used to find out how much more or less one number is, in comparison to another. In adult life we often work out differences, for example, when we note down the mileage before and after a journey to work out the distance travelled.

▶ Children first need to be familiar with language relating to the size of the numbers – fewer, greater, more, less and so on – before they tackle such tasks. They should be encouraged to work practically, matching the members of each set and then counting the unmatched members to find out the difference – how many more or less one set has compared to the other.

▶ To begin with, use real objects to model differences. It is often helpful to arrange them in rows. For example:

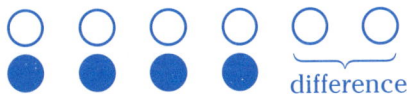

difference

The top set has two more than the other set.

▶ Number lines are also useful for modelling difference:

22   23   (24)   25   26   27   28   29   (30)   31

difference of 6

KEY WORDS

take away

subtract

more than

less than

difference

fewer

the same as

STRATEGIES FOR SOLVING THE TASKS

▶ Adults solve all of these types of tasks using a variety, or combination, of methods:
• we 'just know', since we have an accumulation of number facts or 'bonds' stored in our brains;
• we count or add on;
• we visualise;
• we mentally take apart numbers and perform an operation on part of them, before putting them back together again; for example: we know 7 – 4 = 3, so 17 – 4 must = 13.

▶ When the task is too difficult or time-consuming to calculate mentally, we use a calculator, pencil and paper, or objects to help us.

▶ Children need to develop a repertoire of strategies, so that they can select the most appropriate way to tackle each task. To build up this range, they need to discuss, compare and try out ideas. They should be encouraged to use a variety of mathematical resources. They should learn how to use structured counting apparatus, number lines, grids and cards, as well as calculators, pencil-and-paper, and real object methods.

Curriculum links

This chart outlines the particular strands and statements from each of the UK curriculum documents for maths that apply to the content of this book.

   The processes outlined opposite show how this maths is applied to a range of contexts and how outcomes are reported.

MATHEMATICS IN THE NATIONAL CURRICULUM (ENGLAND AND WALES)

This book covers the following statements from the Key Stage 1 Programme of Study for Number:
▶ Pupils should be given opportunities to:
• develop flexible methods of working with number, orally and mentally;
• use a variety of practical resources and contexts;
• use calculators as a means to explore number;
• record in a variety of ways, including ways that relate to their mental work. (1a, c, d [part] and e)

Pupils should be taught to:
▶ Developing an understanding of place value
• count orally to 10 and beyond, knowing the number names; count collections of objects, checking the total; count in steps of different sizes. (2a [part])
▶ Understanding relationships between numbers and developing methods of computation
• explore and record patterns in addition and subtraction. (3b [part])
▶ Solving numerical problems
• understand the operations of addition, subtraction as taking away and comparison, and the relationship between them, recognise situations to which they apply and use them to solve problems with whole numbers, including situations involving money. (4a)

MATHEMATICS 5–14 (SCOTTISH GUIDELINES)

This book covers the following strands of the Attainment Outcome Number, Money and Measurement:
▶ Add and subtract:
• **Add and subtract:** mentally for numbers 0 to 10, in applications in number, measurement and money, including payments and change to 10p (Level A).
▶ Patterns and sequences:
• **Work with patterns and sequences:** simple number sequences (Level A);
• **Work with patterns and sequences:** whole number sequences within 100 (eg 10, 15, 20..., or 89, 79, 69...) (Level B).

NORTHERN IRELAND CURRICULUM FOR MATHEMATICS

This book covers the following strands of Number from the Programme of Study at Key Stage 1:
▶ Operations and their application
Pupils should have opportunities to:
(a) understand the operations of addition and subtraction, add and subtract, initially using small numbers, use these skills to solve number problems involving whole numbers;
(c) know addition and subtraction facts initially to 10, and then to 20.
▶ Pupils should use calculators to explore, through play and number games, how a calculator works and how it can be used as a tool for calculating with realistic data.

Using and applying

All of the activities in **Maths Focus** involve applying mathematics. This chart will help you to identify which strands of Using and Applying Mathematics are part of each activity. Problem-solving and Enquiry (Scottish 5–14 Guidelines) and Processes (NI Curriculum) are also addressed through these statements.

Activities	Problem Solving	Communication	Logical Reasoning
DIAGNOSTIC ASSESSMENT			
Teddy bears' picnic	Selects a different outcome to others in the group. Uses all the items in the set. Explains the solution in words.	Talks about the work. Answers simple, direct questions. Records the arrangement.	Begins to spot links with number.
Teddy bears' march	Chooses an appropriate strategy and uses it. Creates several arrangements.	Answers questions you ask. Talks to his or her partner while working on the task. Records pictorially or symbolically.	Counts the bears. Works systematically. Calculates hidden objects.
ASSESSMENT DOUBLE-CHECK			
Postman Pat	Knows how to tackle the problem. Works systematically. Checks results. Completes the task.	Knows how to use the symbols. Explains the story of the statements clearly. Records clearly and systematically.	Shows understanding of the relationship between individual statements (not having to count all the letters each time).
REINFORCEMENT ACTIVITIES			
Fill the bucket – empty the bucket	Talk about what the game involves. Play the game and know when it is finished.	Talk about how the game is played. Record the game in his or her own way, and explain it.	See the relationship between subtraction and addition: 'What will happen if two are taken away, and then two are added?'
Ten green bottles	Work systematically.	Record findings in own way. Explain the recording.	Order the work carefully. Discuss patterns.
In the shop	Discuss strategies to work out change. Try out different strategies.	Verbalise strategies, or draw a picture to show workings.	
Lost your marbles	Try out all of the strategies suggested. Check results.	Explain method of recording. Discuss different methods.	Order their work.
In my hand	Use strategies to find out the missing number. Try out strategies to find the best.	Explain recording.	Check results before opening his or her hand.
Jump!	Use the appropriate maths to decide on the best move.	See '+' as 'going forwards' and '–' as 'going backwards'. Discuss strategies. Explain recordings.	Understand why the deadlock happens.
Going up the wall	Arrange the counters neatly to see at a glance who has the most/fewest.	Use relevant vocabulary to talk about the game.	
Tower blocks	Select the appropriate operation. Check instructions practically.	Explain how he or she is working out the instructions. Select the appropriate symbol (+/–).	
Spotted dogs	Discuss strategies.	Use the vocabulary 'one more' and 'one less'.	Explain the pattern in the sequence of numbers and predict the next sequence.
ENRICHMENT ACTIVITIES			
The register	Check work.	Talk about what is involved. Explain recordings.	Use the work to predict the answers.
Toppling towers	Select the appropriate maths to solve the task.	Discuss methods of recording the working-out.	Predict the answers by organising findings into a table.
Only 5 left	Work systematically. Select an appropriate method to solve the task.	Talk about what is involved. Discuss methods with the group.	Look for number patterns.
The biscuit tin	Select the maths to work out the difference.	Use 'more than' and 'less than'.	Work out the difference.
Countdown	Calculate in his or her head.	Explain method of recording. Explain the rules of the game.	Develop a strategy for winning.
What's next?		Discuss what is involved.	Record the patterns. Predict the next number in the sequence.

Teddy bears

For 'Teddy bears' picnic':
▶ *'What can you tell me about your arrangement?'*
▶ *'Which of your rugs has the most teddy bears?'*
▶ *'How many teddy bears are there altogether?'*
▶ *'Is your arrangement different to everyone else's?'*

For 'Teddy bears' march':
▶ *'How many can you see now?'*
▶ *'How many do you think your partner can see?'*

HERE'S THE MATHS

▶ The children may automatically use their understanding of subtraction to say how many bears are on the other rug or other side of the screen. For example, they may say: 'There are six altogether, and two on this rug, so that leaves four on the other rug.'

Key aims

▶ To discover how confident the child is about:
• partitioning a set of six;
• counting a number of objects;
• subtraction by counting on to a given total.

What you need

▶ at least 2 copies of the 'Teddy bears' picnic' activity sheet and 1 copy of 'Teddy bears' march' sheet for each child
▶ scissors, glue
▶ 6 plastic teddy bears per child (optional)
▶ piece of A5 card per pair

Organisation

▶ For 'Teddy bears' picnic' each child will be choosing their own picnic arrangement, so can be assessed individually.
▶ 'Teddy bears' march' requires children to work in pairs, but each child must be assessed on a one-to-one basis.

The activity

▶ Give out the 'Teddy bears' picnic' activity sheets. Explain to the children that they are going to find places for the bears to sit down for a picnic. If you are not using plastic teddy bears, let each child cut out the teddy bears at the foot of their page.
▶ Ask them to seat the teddy bears on the two rugs. Tell them to find a different way from others in the group. Ask each child how many bears are on each rug and how many altogether. You could ask them which rug has more. Let them stick down the cut-out bears to record their arrangement and write down the numbers to show how many.
▶ Let them repeat the task for a different seating arrangement.
▶ If they complete this confidently, give pairs 'Teddy bears' march'. Ask them to sit one on each side of the line of bears with a screen made from a piece of A5 card between them.
▶ Show them how to divide the line of bears into two sections using the screen. Each child will be able to see a different set of bears on their side (see example on sheet).
▶ Talk through an example by asking both children (in turn) to say how many teddy bears they can see.
▶ Tell them to move the screen to different places and, if appropriate for their experience, to record the outcomes.

Where next?

▶ If a child completes both activities easily, you will need to try an assessment at a higher level.

Teddy bears' picnic

Arrange the teddy bears on the two rugs.

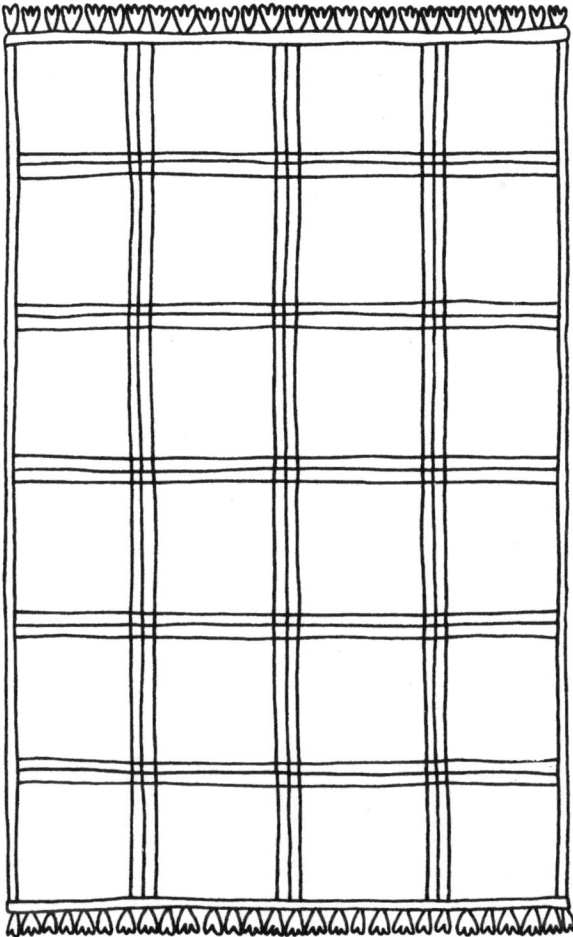

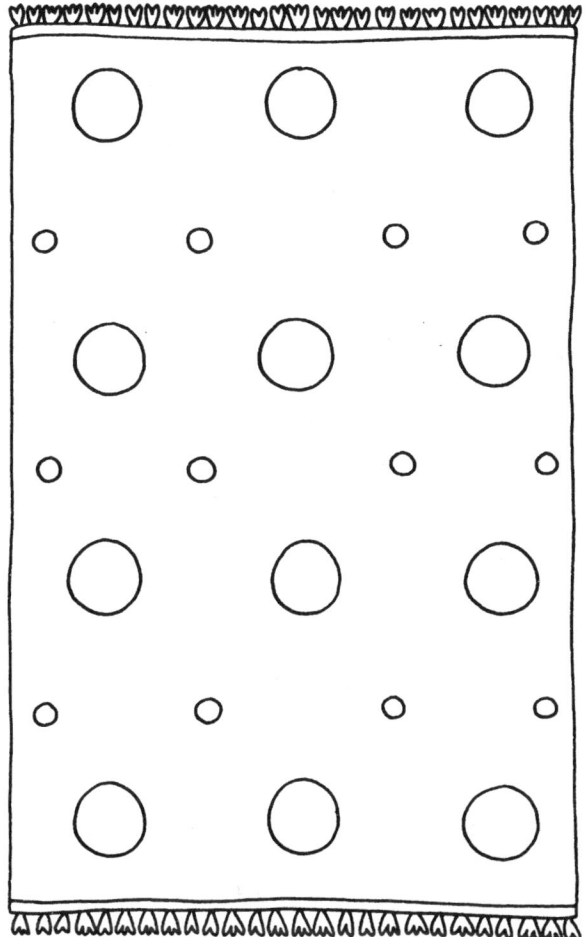

For 'Teddy bears' picnic':
PROBLEM SOLVING
▶ Does the child:
• select a different outcome to others in the group?
• use all of the items in the set?
• explain the solution in words?
COMMUNICATION
▶ Can the child:
• talk about the work?
• answer simple, direct questions?
• record the arrangement?
LOGICAL REASONING
▶ Does the child begin to spot links with number?

For 'Teddy bears' march':
PROBLEM SOLVING
▶ Can the child:
• choose an appropriate strategy and use it?
• create several arrangements?
COMMUNICATION
▶ Does the child:
• answer questions you ask?
• talk to his or her partner while working on the task?
• record pictorially or symbolically?
LOGICAL REASONING
▶ Can the child:
• count the bears?
• work systematically?
• calculate hidden objects?

Assessing understanding

▶ Look for the following to indicate that the children are ready for **Enrichment activities**. They may:
• say confidently how many teddy bears are on each rug;
• tell you how many there are altogether;
• recognise which rug holds more (if unequal);
• observe that their arrangement is different to others;
• record under each rug the number of teddy bears;
• tell you confidently how many bears they can see on their side of the screen and predict how many their partner can see;
• tell you how they worked it out;
• find a range of arrangements;
• record with pictures or mathematical symbols;
• work systematically on the task.
▶ Look for the following to indicate that the children are in need of more work on the concepts of subtraction and addition. They may:
• be unable to talk about their rugs;
• not seat all six teddy bears;
• be unable to count accurately the number on each rug;
• be unable to count to six;
• be unable to find a strategy to predict how many bears their partner has on their side of the screen;
• be unsure how to record their work;
• be unable to relate the mathematics to this concept.

Children who need more help

▶ If any children are lacking in confidence, or are having difficulty completing the activities, offer them a smaller number of teddy bears. You may need to work closely with these children to clarify whether their difficulty relates to the level at which the task is pitched or to the complexity of the language.
▶ If the children are having difficulty with the hidden teddy bears, use a sheet of Perspex or acetate for the screen so that they can see both sides.
▶ You may need to take some children through the 'Teddy bears' march' task systematically by yourself, moving the partition to generate the bonds of six.
▶ For children who need help with basic number recognition, you could try the **Reinforcement activity** 'Postman Pat' (page 14). This activity also introduces subtraction.
▶ All the **Reinforcement activities** up to page 25 address 'taking away from a set'.
▶ 'Fill the bucket...' (page 16) and 'Jump!' (page 26) introduce and reinforce the concept of '+' and '−'.
▶ For children who find the comparison of sets difficult, you could try the **Reinforcement activities** 'Going up the wall' (page 28) or 'Tower blocks' (page 30). 'Spotted dogs' on page 32 goes on to look at 'one more' and 'one less'.

Name _____

Teddy bears' march

I can see 4 bears

I can see 2 bears

How many bears on your side?

How will you record this?

Postman Pat

Key aims

▶ To assess if the child understands:
• how to subtract from a set;
• the meaning of '–' and '=' symbols;
• how to construct a number statement for a subtraction.

What you need

▶ 1 activity sheet per child
▶ pencils
▶ 1 dice marked 1, 2, 3, 1, 2 3 per child
▶ set of number and operation cards per child (see page 46)

Organisation

▶ Write in a number of letters in the sack on each child's activity sheet as appropriate for his/her ability level.

Introduction

▶ You may want first to read one of the *Postman Pat* books by John Cunliffe (Hippo) with the children.

The activity

▶ Give out the activity sheets and number cards.
▶ Ask the children to draw in the sack on their sheet the number of letters that Pat has. Ask them to find the number card which shows how many letters in Pat's sack. They then shake their dice to tell Pat how many letters to deliver to the first house. They cross out these letters in the sack and make a number sentence with the cards to show what they have done and record it on the sheet.
▶ Leave them to continue until all the letters are 'delivered'.

Assessing understanding

▶ Look for:
• ability to work quickly and confidently;
• confidence in working mentally.

Where next?

▶ If the children show confidence in working with numbers up to 10, let them repeat the activity with a higher number of letters.
▶ If the children still lack confidence, they will need further **Reinforcement activities** before they tackle problems set in less visual and practical contexts, or using larger numbers.

ASSESSING USING & APPLYING

PROBLEM SOLVING
▶ Does the child:
• know how to tackle the problem?
• work systematically?
• check results?
• complete the task?
COMMUNICATION
▶ Does the child:
• know how to use the symbols?
• explain the story of the statements clearly?
▶ record clearly and systematically?
LOGICAL REASONING
▶ Does the child show understanding of the relationship between individual statements (not having to count all the letters each time)?

TALK ABOUT

▶ *'What is the story of this statement?'*
▶ *'How do you know this is the right number of letters to deliver?'*
▶ *'How are you working out how many letters are left?'*

HERE'S THE MATHS

▶ By writing in the number of letters on each child's sack you have the flexiblity to assess subtraction using numbers below or above 10.

Name _____

Postman Pat

Throw the dice to tell Pat how many letters to deliver.
Write number sentences to show how many letters Pat has left.

Pat has ☐ letters in his sack.

My number sentences:

PROBLEM SOLVING
▶ Talk about what the game involves.
▶ Play the game and know when it is finished.
COMMUNICATION
▶ Talk about how the game is played.
▶ Record the game in his or her own way, and explain it.
LOGICAL REASONING
▶ See the relationship between subtraction and addition: 'What will happen if two are taken away, and then two are added?'

TALK ABOUT

▶ *'How many must you put in before you win?'*
▶ *'Which number do you need to win?'*
▶ *'When you've taken two out, how many will be left?'*
▶ *'What if the adder rolls the same number as you?'*

HERE'S THE MATHS

▶ Children can physically see from this activity that addition makes numbers greater and subtraction makes them smaller.

WHAT TO LOOK FOR

▶ Does the child understand the effect of adding and subtracting?
▶ Can the child predict what she needs to do to win?

MORE HELP NEEDED

▶ Some children may not count the beans accurately. Encourage them to count out loud as they have their turn. Get them to concentrate on the counting rather than the idea of adding or subtracting.

REINFORCEMENT ACTIVITY

Fill the bucket – empty the bucket

Key aims

▶ To reinforce the concept of subtraction as taking some away.
▶ To reinforce the concept of addition as adding some on.
▶ **Also covered:** introducing the concept of addition and subtraction as inverse operations, or 'having the opposite effect to each other'.

What you need

▶ 1 activity sheet per pair
▶ 1 small bucket per pair
▶ bean bags per pair
▶ a one and two dot, or numeral, dice per pair

The activity

▶ Talk through the instructions on the activity sheet and then ask the children if they can work out how to play the game.
▶ They need to see that the adder puts bean bags in the bucket on her turn. Then the subtractor throws the dice and takes that number of bean bags out. Make sure they realise that for this game ten bags in the bucket means that it is full.
▶ When you are sure they understand the rules leave them to play the game.

Extension ideas

▶ Devise a way to record the game.
▶ Change the rules in some way to make a new game. For example, using a dice marked +0, +1, +2, +3, −1, −2 both players could aim to fill the bucket. The winner is the first to fill it.
▶ Use more bean bags, say 20, and play with a 1–6 dice.

Name _____

Fill the bucket – empty the bucket

You will need:

bucket

bean bags

dice

two people

Start with the bucket half full.

Decide who will be the adder and who will be the subtractor.

Take it in turns to throw the dice to have your go.

The subtractor wins when the bucket is **empty**.

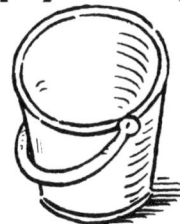

The adder wins when the bucket is **full**.

Swap over and play again!

Ten green bottles

Key aims

▶ To introduce or clarify subtraction from 10.
▶ To use simple counting on to find out how many objects have been subtracted.

What you need

▶ at least 1 activity sheet and 1 postermat (or several copies of page 48) per two or three children
▶ dry-wipe markers and wipers
▶ pencils and plain paper
▶ coloured paper, scissors, adhesive

Introduction

Sing 'Ten green bottles' beforehand with the class.
Ten green bottles standing on a wall,
Ten green bottles standing on a wall,
And if one green bottle should accidentally fall,
There'll be nine green bottles standing on the wall... .

The activity

▶ Remind the children of the song. Give out the activity sheets, postermats/page 48 and dry-wipe marker pens.
▶ Ask the children to draw ten bottles on the postermat wall.
▶ Ask them how many bottles would be left on the wall if one fell off. Let them show this on the postermat and then record what they have done on their activity sheet. Some children may draw, write, or make marks to represent the bottles or use numbers to show the recording. Encourage them to use their own ideas.
▶ Now ask them to wipe the postermat clean and start again but this time have a different number of bottles falling off.
▶ Tell them to continue with one child drawing the bottles on the wall, and the other(s) wiping so many off and drawing these on the floor and then together recording what they have done. They should check that there is a total of ten bottles drawn on the postermat each time.
▶ Stay with the children until they know what to do.
▶ They may want more copies of the activity sheet to do permanent recording.

Extension ideas

▶ Ask the children to say a number sentence for each picture, or use number and operation cards to show the sentence.
▶ Sing a version of 'Ten green bottles' where the number of bottles that fall off varies.

USING & APPLYING

PROBLEM SOLVING
▶ Work systematically.
COMMUNICATION
▶ Record findings in own way.
▶ Explain the recording.
LOGICAL REASONING
▶ Order the work carefully.
▶ Discuss patterns seen.

TALK ABOUT

▶ *'How can you work out how many have fallen off?'*
▶ *'Have you found all the ways of doing it?'*
▶ *'You've had one bottle fall off, and two and three. What's next?'*
▶ *'What patterns can you see?'*

HERE'S THE MATHS

▶ When you ask the children how they are working out how many bottles have fallen off they may suggest counting on – mentally, with their fingers, or as they draw – or say they just know, because, for example, 4 + 6 = 10.
▶ When you ask the children to look for patterns encourage them to look at the descending order of the first column of numbers:

$$10 + 0 = 10$$
$$9 + 1 = 10$$
$$8 + 2 = 10 \text{ and so on.}$$

WHAT TO LOOK FOR

▶ Can the child start from a number and count on to 10, keeping track of how many bottles he is counting?

MORE HELP NEEDED

▶ Some children will have difficulty counting on from a number. They need to play games using two dice, one with numbers on and one with dots. Jumping on and back on a floor number line also helps.

Name _____

Ten green bottles

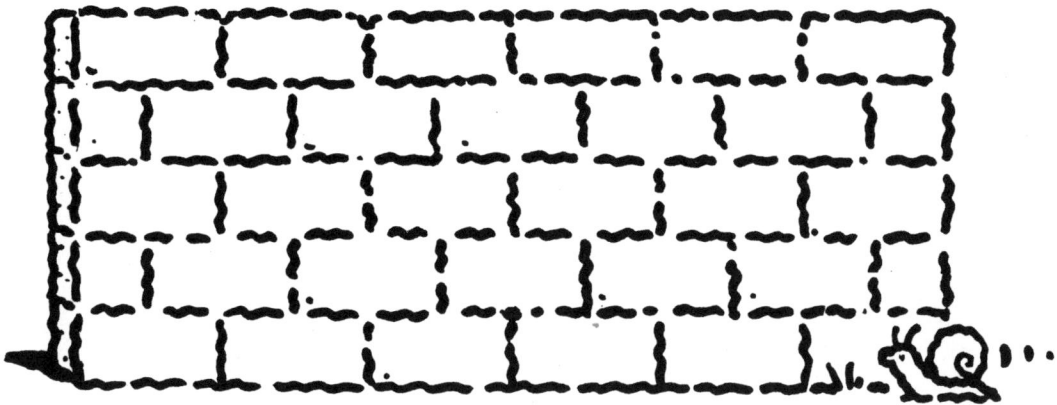

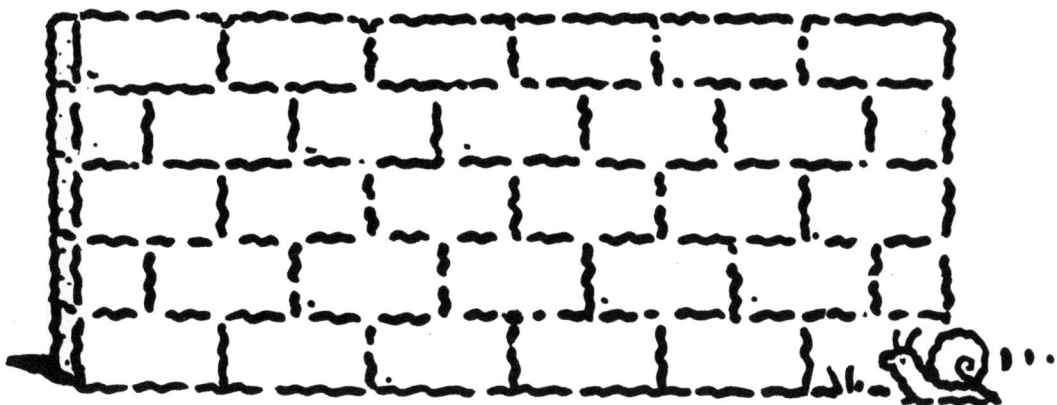

In the shop

Key aims

▶ To introduce or clarify stages for working out how many objects have been taken from a set.
▶ To use subtraction in a real-life context.

What you need

▶ objects to buy
▶ 10 × 1p for each child (in real pennies)
▶ price tags, pens
▶ 1 activity sheet per child

Organisation

▶ If you don't already have one in your classroom, set up a simple play shop – this can be done quite quickly.
▶ Ask the children to write price tags for values up to 10p for the articles on sale.
▶ Give each child ten pennies and allow them to play in the shop before they begin the activity.

The activity

▶ Ask the children to check that they each have ten pennies. Go into the shop and take the role of the shopkeeper.
▶ Let each child in turn come to buy something and tell you how much money is left once she has made a purchase.
▶ When each child has bought something, ask them if they can think of how they could work out how much they have left before they buy. They may suggest grouping the money in their hand or counting on. Offer and explain these, if they do not suggest them.
▶ Go back into the shop and this time ask the child to tell you how much money they will have left before you give the change. Encourage them just to look at the money in their hand and work it out without moving the coins, so that they work mentally.
▶ Give out the activity sheets. Explain that they are going to choose an item to buy from the shop, fill in the price tag on the sheet and then work out how much money is left. Show them that they should record this in the purse on the right-hand side.

Extension ideas

▶ Let them try to buy something else from the shop with their left-over money.
▶ Let them try using a mixture of 2p and 1p coins with which to buy things.

USING & APPLYING

PROBLEM SOLVING
▶ Discuss strategies to work out change.
▶ Try out different strategies.
COMMUNICATION
▶ Verbalise strategies, or draw a picture to show workings.

TALK ABOUT

▶ 'How much money do you think you will have left this time?'
▶ 'How are you working it out?'
▶ 'Which item left you with the most change?'

HERE'S THE MATHS

▶ This activity uses money for the take away aspect of subtraction. Counting is the simplest strategy to work out the change, although using knowledge of number patterns is quickest.
▶ When you ask children to explain how they are working it out many will comment: 'I am doing it/thinking in my head.' If so, ask them: 'What can you see in your head?'

WHAT TO LOOK FOR

▶ Does the child count on from what he has spent up to the 10p to find the change?
▶ Does the child say he 'just knows' because he is familiar with the patterns of the numbers?

MORE HELP NEEDED

▶ Have pennies or counters available for children having difficulty working it out in their heads.
▶ Develop counting skills by arranging a set of objects in different ways and looking at the patterns.

Name _____

In the shop...
How much money will I have left?

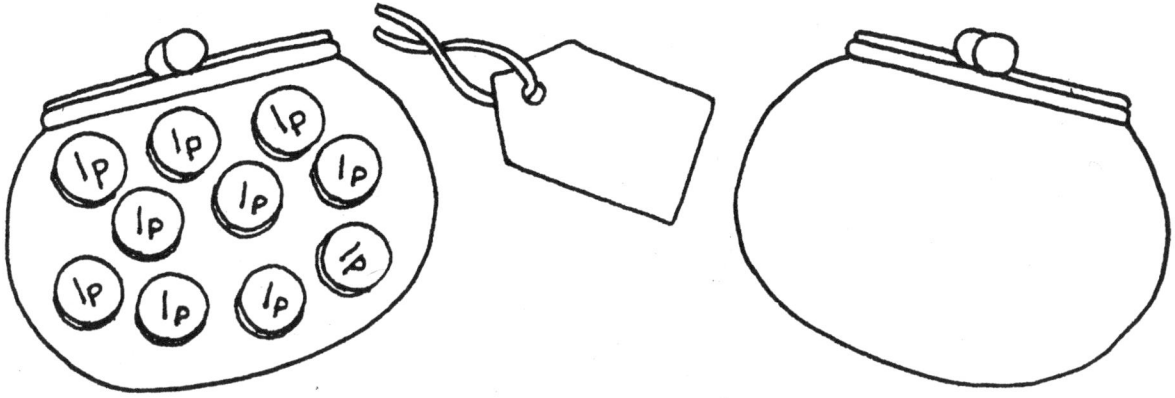

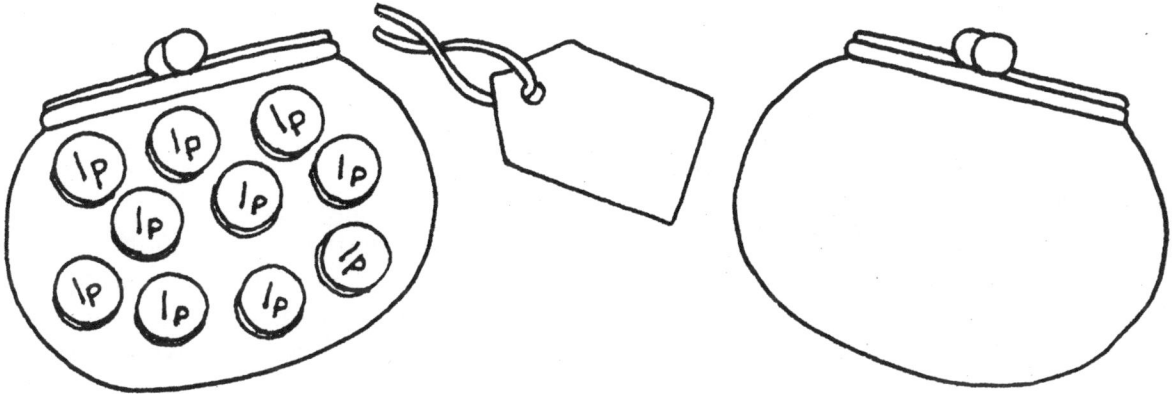

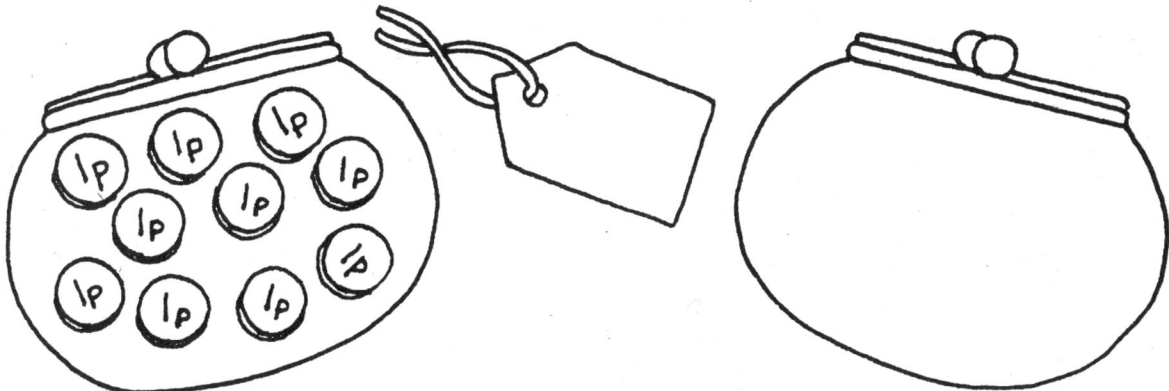

Lost your marbles

Key aims

▶ To introduce or clarify strategies for working out how many objects have been taken from a set.
▶ To develop methods of recording.

What you need

▶ 1 activity sheet per child
▶ pencils and paper

The activity

▶ Give out the activity sheets and ask the children how many marbles the girl is holding. Then point to the speech bubble and ask them how many she had before (ten).
▶ Talk about ways of finding out how many she has lost. They may suggest:
• counting on;
• using the marble number line at the bottom of the page;
• making a picture in their heads;
• drawing a picture of ten marbles and crossing six off;
• drawing more marbles until they have a total of ten;
• they just know, because, for example, 6 + 4 = 10.
Offer and explain some of these, if the children have not suggested them.
▶ Try out the different strategies, as a group.
▶ Look at the other hands on the sheet, and explain that in each case there were ten marbles to start with. Tell them that they are going to work out how many marbles have been lost in each case. Encourage them to use their own methods, and to record their thinking.
▶ Leave them to complete the sheet.

Extension ideas

▶ Put the hands in order, from the one with most marbles left.
▶ Make number statements to go with each picture, for example, 10 − 6 = 4.
▶ Use the postermat to explore the number of snails which have gone from the wall by morning when there was always 15 to start with. For example, how many have crawled away if there are 12 left?
▶ Create a poster, displaying the various methods the children used and talk about the different methods.

USING & APPLYING

PROBLEM SOLVING
▶ Try out all of the strategies suggested.
▶ Check results.
COMMUNICATION
▶ Explain method of recording.
▶ Discuss different methods.
LOGICAL REASONING
▶ Order their work.

TALK ABOUT

▶ 'How could we find out how many marbles she has lost?'
▶ 'How do you know it's right? How could you check?'
▶ 'Did everyone use the same method?'
▶ 'Can you see how Sarah worked it out?'
▶ 'Why is it easy to see what Jacinta has done?'

HERE'S THE MATHS

▶ The children need to either count on or use a mental image of how numbers are made up to solve the task. Using fingers as counters is a good strategy.
▶ If they set out the hands in order, they may be able to predict some answers using the number patterns.

WHAT TO LOOK FOR

▶ Does the child count on to find the answer?
▶ Does the child draw in the missing marbles to make up ten?
▶ Does the child 'just know'?

MORE HELP NEEDED

▶ Some children may not know how to begin solving the task. Encourage them to see it in their mind and practically. Take ten marbles and cover the 'lost' ones with your hand. Together count how many are left. Give them more practice in building up mental images of numbers.

Name _____

Lost your marbles

I had 10.

How many are lost?

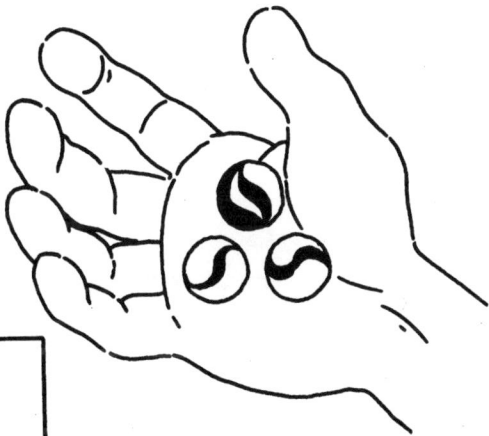

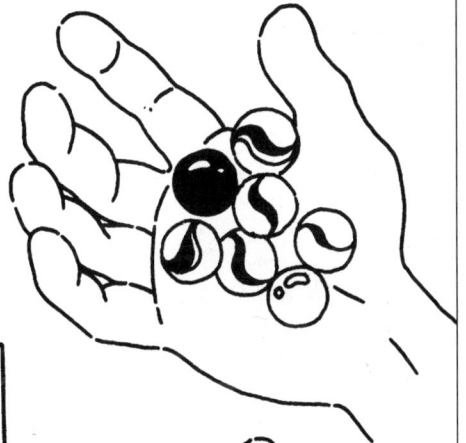

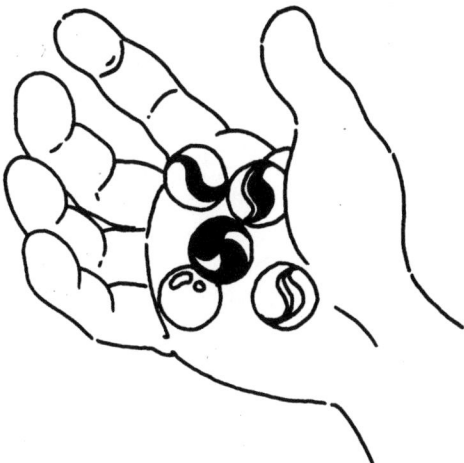

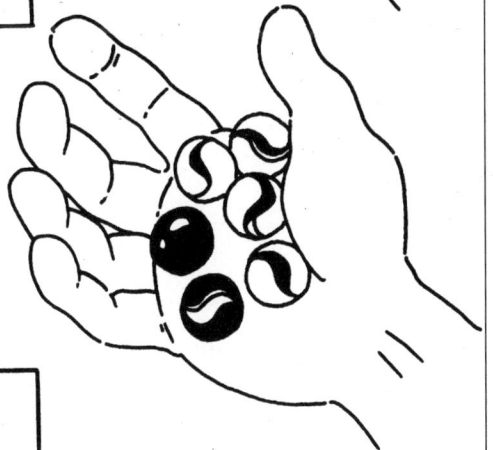

How many are lost?

1 2 3 4 5 6 7 8 9 10

In my hand

USING & APPLYING

PROBLEM SOLVING
▶ Use strategies to find out the missing number.
▶ Try out strategies to find the best.
COMMUNICATION
▶ Explain recording.
LOGICAL REASONING
▶ Check results before opening his or her hand.

TALK ABOUT

▶ *'How do you know you have the right number for the number of beans hidden in the hand? How can you check?'*
▶ *'How are you working it out?'*
▶ *'Can you get all the number pairs possible for making 5?'*
▶ *'How will you record these?'*

HERE'S THE MATHS

▶ To find out the missing number of beans each time the children need to count on or use their knowledge of number patterns.
▶ To check whether they have got the correct number of beans missing they need to add their guess to the visible number to see if it comes to five.

WHAT TO LOOK FOR

▶ Does the child count on to find the answer?
▶ Does the child 'just know' what it will be?

MORE HELP NEEDED

▶ Children who don't know where to start to solve the task need more activities which help them to develop mental images of number patterns.

Key aim

▶ To clarify strategies for working out how many objects have been taken from a set.

What you need

▶ 5 and 10 number cards (page 46)
▶ pencils and plain paper
▶ 1 activity sheet per child
▶ 10 beans/counters per child

Organisation

▶ Make sure that the beans or counters you use are small enough to fit in a child's hand.

The activity

▶ Invite the children to play a number game. To play the game, show the children the five beans in your hand, and display the number card for '5'. Place two of the beans on the table and close your hand around the remaining beans so that the children can't see them.
▶ Ask them how many beans they think you are hiding and how they could work it out. They may suggest:
• counting on mentally, or using their fingers;
• using their five fingers to represent the five beans and taking two away by bending two fingers down.
Offer and explain these, if they have not suggested them.
▶ Invite the children to identify the two numbers related to that group of five beans: the number of beans that is visible, and the number that is in your hand. Verify these two numbers by counting the total to check that it makes five.
▶ Give out the activity sheets and explain that they are going to work out how many beans are hidden in the hand each time. Let them use the beans to help them if they want to.
▶ Make sure they realise that the number between the hands indicates how many beans the person has in total – either 5 or 10. You may want together to go through one of the examples where ten beans are involved. Show them where to record the number of beans missing (the square in the bottom corner).
▶ Leave them to complete the activity sheet.

Extension ideas

▶ In pairs, investigate all the possibilities for five beans, using their own method to record their work.
▶ Try a different total number of beans, recording the work.

Name _____

In my hand

I've got 5 beans.
How many are hidden
in my hand?

How many in my hand?

5	5
10	10
5	5
10	10

USING & APPLYING

PROBLEM SOLVING
▶ Use the appropriate maths to decide on the best move.
COMMUNICATION
▶ See '+' as 'going forwards' and '–' as 'going backwards'.
▶ Discuss strategies.
▶ Explain recordings.
LOGICAL REASONING
▶ Understand why the deadlock happens.

TALK ABOUT

▶ *'What should the jumper do if I hold up this card?'*
▶ *'How does the jumper know which way to jump?'*
▶ *'How many jumps is it to 10?'*
▶ *'What happens if both teams use the highest card each time?'*
▶ *'Can you change the game, to prevent this happening?'*

HERE'S THE MATHS

▶ In working out the jumps from one number to another, make sure the children do not count the number the jumper is on.
▶ To help the children to understand why the deadlock occurs, take away all of the number cards except one. The jumper will be back on the 5 after each team has had a turn.

WHAT TO LOOK FOR

▶ Does the child look for strategies?
▶ Does the child understand how to add or subtract on the number line?

MORE HELP NEEDED

▶ Children having difficulty with the number line need structured activities using a floor number line, or playing games moving toy people along a number line according to a rule.

Jump!

Key aims

▶ To introduce or clarify use of +/– symbols in the context of a number line.
▶ To discriminate between '+' and '–'.
▶ **Also covered**: '+' and '–' as inverse or 'opposite' operations.

What you need

▶ 0–10 floor number line
▶ 2 sets of large number cards from 0–4 and '+' and '-' operation cards (could be enlarged from the cards on page 46)
▶ at least 1 activity sheet per group
▶ coloured pens

Organisation

▶ Lay out the number line – you could use rubber-backed number tiles, or tape or chalk numbers on to the floor. Make sure all the children can see the numbers the right way up.

The activity

▶ Choose one child to be the 'jumper' and ask him or her to stand on number 5 on the floor number line. Group the remaining children into two teams and give each team a set of the number and operation cards.
▶ Explain that one team has to get the jumper to the number 10, and the other to 0, but they're not allowed to talk to the jumper. Instead, each team takes a turn at holding up some cards to tell the jumper what to do.
▶ When the jumper reaches 0 or 10, she swaps with a member of the winning team and the game can begin again.
▶ Ask them to use the activity sheet to record the moves made each time. Let them decide on their own methods of recording. They may decide to use a different colour pen to distinguish between each team.
▶ When they have played for a while ask the children which is the best card to use. They may suggest:
• choosing the highest number card;
• always using the '+' in one team, '–' in the other.
If they reach this latter strategy quite soon, the game will end in a deadlock each time. If they don't realise the strategy themselves, offer and explain it and allow them to play again.

Extension idea

▶ Change the rules of the game to avoid it ending in deadlock each time. They may suggest using different number cards or using a dice to give the move.

Name _____

Jump!

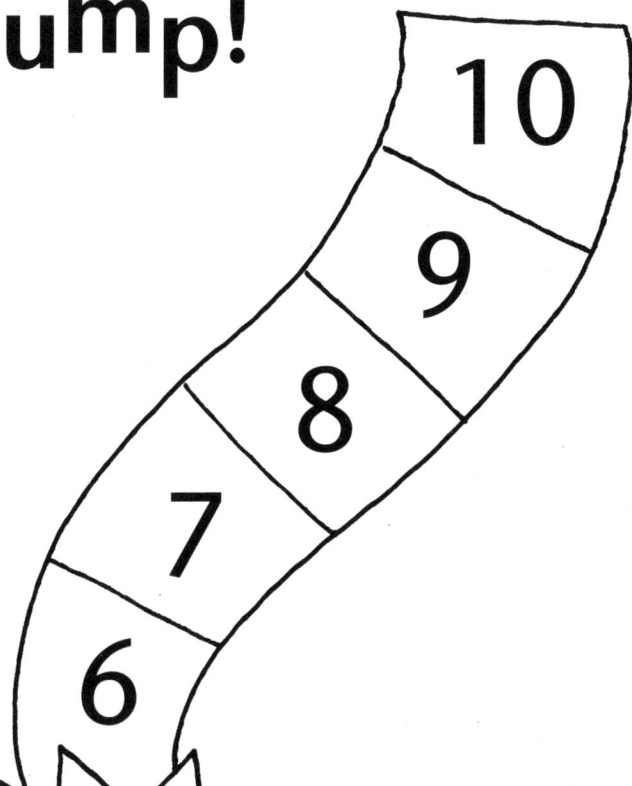

10

9

8

7

6

Start 5

4

3

2

1

0

Going up the wall

USING & APPLYING

PROBLEM SOLVING
▶ Arrange the counters neatly to see at a glance who has the most/fewest.
COMMUNICATION
▶ Use relevant vocabulary to talk about the game.

TALK ABOUT

▶ 'Which player won that time?'
▶ 'How many more did you have?'
▶ 'Why did you win that round?'

HERE'S THE MATHS

▶ This activity deals with the difference aspect of subtraction. The children have to decide how many more or fewer they have than the other player. Organising their counters systematically will help them to work it out. Difference can be difficult for children to work out. There is information on this aspect of subtraction in the 'Here's the maths' section on page 6.

WHAT TO LOOK FOR

▶ Can the child organise the counters to show the difference?
▶ Does the child understand the words 'more', 'fewer', 'difference'?
▶ Can the child tell you the difference by 'just knowing'?

MORE HELP NEEDED

▶ Some children may have difficulty organising the counters to find the difference. You could give them interlocking cubes instead of counters so they can join their cubes together to visibly see which player has most/fewest.

Key aims

▶ To compare numbers using difference.
▶ To use vocabulary 'more' and 'fewer'.

What you need

▶ 1 postermat (or copy of page 48) per pair
▶ 10 counters of one colour each (sets in red, blue or black)
▶ 1 more/fewer spinner per pair
▶ 1 activity sheet (or more) per pair
▶ pencils

Organisation

▶ Make the more/fewer spinner from a plastic disc, such as a logic block. Write 'more' (or 'M') on one side and 'fewer' (or 'F') on the other. Let the children practise spinning the disc between their thumb and forefinger before starting the activity.

The activity

▶ Show the children the postermat, pointing out the coloured pathways on the wall. Ask them to trace along the pathways with their fingers.
▶ Explain the game:
• Decide in your pair who will be Player 1 and who will be Player 2 and who will be which colour.
• Each player places their ten 'snails' (counters) on the 'grass' at the bottom of the wall. Each player then moves some (any number) of his counters on to his corresponding colour track on the wall. They then record the number of snails each has on their track on the activity sheet.
• Next one of the players spins the more/fewer spinner and records this on the activity sheet – 'm' for more, 'f' for fewer.
• The winner of that turn is the player who has most/fewest snails depending on the spinner. The winner writes his or her name in one of the boxes at the bottom of the activity sheet.
• When the boxes are all full, both players count up their wins and record them at the bottom. They spin the spinner again to find out who is the overall winner – the one with more wins, or the one with fewer.
▶ Demonstrate one go to make sure the children are sure about what to do.
▶ Leave them to play in their pairs.

Extension idea

▶ Invent their own game using the spinner and a dice.

Name _____

Going up the wall

Player 1		Player 2	Player 1		Player 2
☐	◯	☐	☐	◯	☐

Player 1		Player 2	Player 1		Player 2
☐	◯	☐	☐	◯	☐

Player 1		Player 2	Player 1		Player 2
☐	◯	☐	☐	◯	☐

Player 1		Player 2
☐	◯	☐

Write your name in a box, when you win:

Count your wins.

Player 1   Player 2

☐   ☐

◯

Spin to win!

_____
_____
_____
_____
_____
_____
_____

Tower blocks

Key aims

▶ To introduce or reinforce the language of number: more, fewer, the same, different.
▶ To use the operator symbols '−' and '+'.

What you need

▶ Multilink/Unifix cubes
▶ blank cards or 'flags'
▶ Blu-Tack
▶ felt-tipped pens
▶ 1 activity sheet per child

The activity

▶ Ask each child to take a handful of cubes and make them into a tower. Talk about which tower has the fewest cubes, whether there are any towers the same, whose tower used the most cubes.
▶ Next select two towers: one with five cubes, the other with more than five. Ask the children to suggest how to make the big tower the same as the smaller one. They may suggest taking away some cubes.
▶ Invite a child to write down the instructions on a flag and stick it on the relevant tower using Blu-Tack, for example, '− 4' on the taller tower. Check to see if the instruction is correct.
▶ Show the children the activity sheet. Explain that they are going to decide what number and sometimes which of the '+' or '−' signs to write in each flag to say how to make that tower five blocks high – the same as the first tower on the sheet.
▶ Explain that then they will make their own towers and add flags to show how to make each five cubes high.
▶ Leave them to complete the activity sheet.

Extension ideas

▶ Invent a tower building game using number dice, or operation and number dice (+0, +1, +2, + 3, −1, −2).
▶ In pairs, make a tower each and take it in turns to give instructions on a flag to tell the other person how to make her tower the same.

USING & APPLYING

PROBLEM SOLVING
▶ Select the appropriate operation.
▶ Check instructions practically.
COMMUNICATION
▶ Explain how she or he is working out the instructions.
▶ Select the appropriate symbol (+/−).

TALK ABOUT

▶ 'How many cubes do you need to add to this tower?'
▶ 'Do you need to add or take away cubes from this tower? How do you know?'

HERE'S THE MATHS

▶ In everyday life the difference form of subtraction occurs more commonly than the take away form. Children see each type as being different and they need practice at each before they realise that they are the same operation.

WHAT TO LOOK FOR

▶ Can the child compare the towers and talk about the difference?
▶ Can the child use the language of comparison, such as 'fewest', 'most', 'same', 'difference'?

MORE HELP NEEDED

▶ Some children may need a lot more discussion on the idea of difference, using real situations such as comparing small quantities of sweets or toys. You may need to introduce language such as 'more than', 'fewer than', 'the difference between', and use it in a variety of contexts, before they are confident to tackle this activity.

Tower blocks

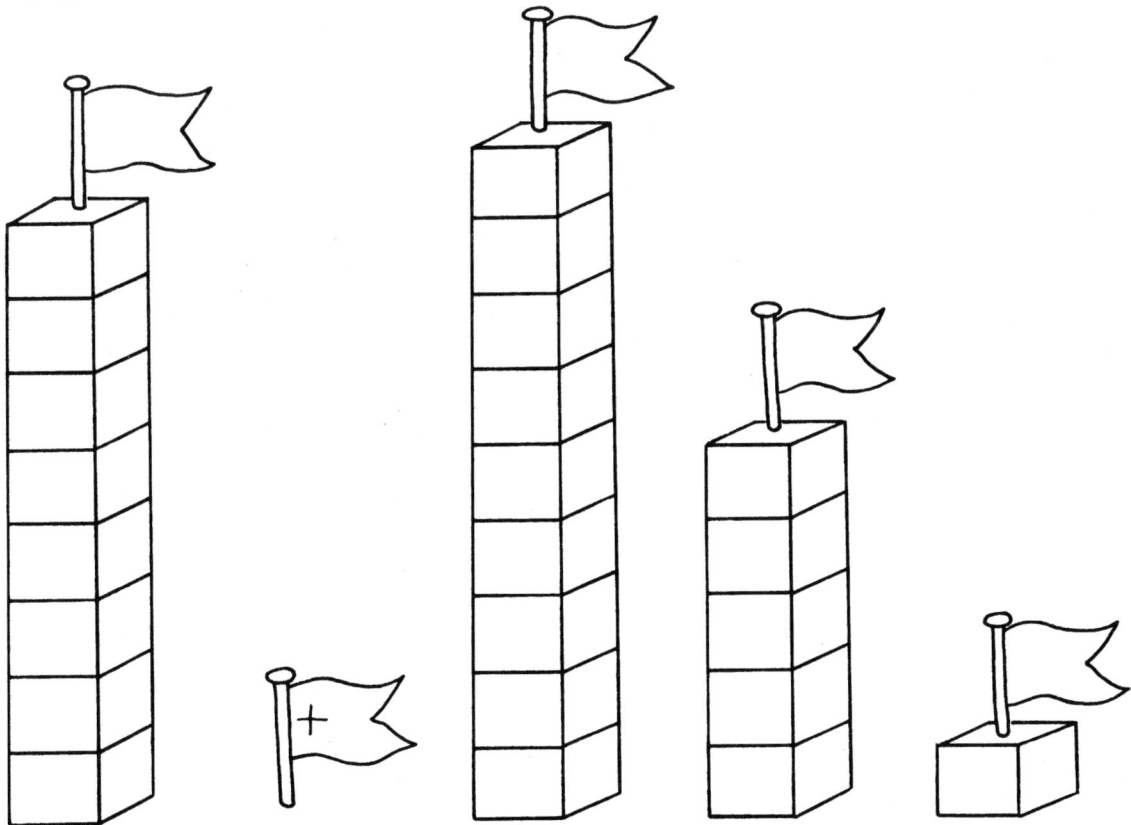

Now make your own towers on the back of this sheet.

Spotted dogs

Key aim

▶ To introduce or clarify 'one more' and 'one less'.

What you need

▶ 1 activity sheet per pair (enlarged to A3 if possible)
▶ about 30 small counters, preferably black, per pair
▶ pencils and plain paper

The activity

▶ Introduce the activity by talking about spotted dogs. The children may have seen the Disney film *101 Dalmatians*. Show them the activity sheet, mentioning that these Dalmatians have no spots yet!
▶ Put up to nine spots (black counters) on to the middle dog and ask the children how many spots they can see on the middle dog.
▶ They then decide how many spots to go on the other dogs, one of which needs one more, the other one fewer.
▶ Explain that they are going to play a game in pairs, taking turns, with one child putting up to nine spots on the middle dog, and the other child putting the correct number of spots on the other dogs so that they have one more or one less.
▶ Ask them to record what they do (on the plain paper).

Extension ideas

▶ Use Multilink to make a tower, and then make two more towers: one with one more cube, the other with one less. Record what they do.
▶ In PE, work in pairs with a pack of 1–10 number cards. One person holds up a card, and the other has to hop/jump/skip and so on one more or one less time than the number shown.

USING & APPLYING

PROBLEM SOLVING
▶ Discuss strategies.
COMMUNICATION
▶ Use the vocabulary 'one more' and 'one less'.
LOGICAL REASONING
▶ Explain the pattern in the sequence of numbers and predict the next sequence.

TALK ABOUT

▶ 'How can you make this dog have one more spot than this dog?'
▶ 'How many spots for the other dog?'
▶ 'How do you know each dog has the correct number of spots?'
▶ 'Can you see a pattern in the numbers?'

HERE'S THE MATHS

▶ This activity gives practice in looking at the pattern of the arrangements of numbers. Encourage the children to use knowledge of number patterns instead of counting the spots.
▶ Explain strategies for counting, including: counting the spots for each dog and checking the numbers are in sequence; matching the counters, except for one; recognising the pattern of the number arrangement.

WHAT TO LOOK FOR

▶ Does the child have to count each time?
▶ Does the child know immediately?

MORE HELP NEEDED

▶ Children having difficulty sequencing the numbers need to put sets of objects in number order.
▶ Children who count painstakingly need practice looking quickly at an arrangement of objects and saying how many there are.

Name _____

Spotted dogs

1 less

1 more

The register

Key aims

▶ To use a number line to solve number problems.
▶ To solve word problems.

What you need

▶ 1 activity sheet per child
▶ a copy of the class register
▶ dry-wipe markers and wipers
▶ a laminated or plastic covered 0–40 number line per pair (see resource sheet on page 47)
▶ pencils and paper

Organisation

▶ Fix a wall number line up near the carpet area so that more children can take part.

Introduction

▶ Involve the children in the maths you do at register time. These real-life number problems give them something to think about while you're busy and will help them to develop strategies to solve the problems.

The activity

▶ Together go through the activity sheet. You may want to talk about your own class register first.
▶ As a group work out how many children are in Mr Jones's class that day. Let them suggest how to work it out from the information given. They may say using counters or pictures, counting on, or back. Let them try out their ideas, and establish the correct answer.
▶ Show them the 0–40 number line and ask one of the children to circle the number of children normally in Mr Jones's class. Show them how to use the marker to jump back the number of absentees, to arrive at the correct answer. Show them how to wipe off the marks to start solving the next one.
▶ Explain that they are going to use their number lines and markers to help them to fill in the missing gaps in the register on the activity sheet. They then record the information as number statements at the bottom of the sheet.

Extension idea

▶ Give the children specific register tasks, for example: *'On Monday, 16 children in Mr Jones's class are having a school lunch, so how many children have packed lunches?'*

Name _____

The register

There are 35 children in the class.
4 children are away.
How many are here?

Help Mr Jones to fill in his register.

	Monday	Tuesday	Wednesday	Thursday	Friday
Away	4			6	
Here		31	33		35

Try to make a number statement for each day.

Toppling towers

USING & APPLYING

PROBLEM SOLVING
▶ Select the appropriate maths to solve the task.
COMMUNICATION
▶ Discuss methods of recording the working-out.
LOGICAL REASONING
▶ Predict the answers by organising findings into a table.

TALK ABOUT

▶ 'How many rods could you take out?'
▶ 'Did it surprise you?'
▶ 'How have you recorded this?'
▶ 'How can you work out how many rods were in the tower just before it fell?'

HERE'S THE MATHS

▶ This activity involves different types of subtraction: take away, difference, and counting on and back. Children can use all three in solving the problem, or use whichever they feel most comfortable with.

WHAT TO LOOK FOR

▶ Does the child use a variety of strategies?
▶ Can the child keep track of the numbers as they play the game?
▶ Does the child count on, compare to find the difference, or take away one by one?
▶ Does the child use knowledge of number patterns to solve the task?

MORE HELP NEEDED

▶ Some children will painstakingly count from the beginning each time. They need more work with smaller numbers, looking at patterns and working on different types of subtraction problems.

Key aims

▶ To clarify 'one less' with numbers larger than 10.
▶ To work out word problems, using subtraction and addition.

What you need

▶ 24 wooden rods – Cuisenaire, colour factor or square dowel – each 6cm long
▶ 1 activity sheet per child
▶ pencils and paper

The activity

▶ Give out the activity sheets and ask the children what they think they have to do.
▶ Together work through the instructions. Let the children set up the tower, taking turns to put a rod in place. Make sure that they leave spaces between the rods, as shown on the picture – this helps to make it more stable.
▶ When they have played the game and the tower has toppled, let them work out from their pile of rods removed how many would have been left in the tower before it fell.
▶ Leave them to play the game a few times, recording the outcome each time, in their own way.
▶ Bring the group back together to share methods used for working out the answers. They may suggest:
• counting on;
• drawing the 24 rods and crossing off the number removed;
• using the pattern 25, 24, 23 and so on and counting back the number of rods they removed.
Offer and explain some of these, if the children do not suggest them.

Extension ideas

▶ Investigate what happens if 30 rods or more are used.
▶ Take away two rods each time and see what pattern the numbers make this time.
▶ Make up their own tower problems for friends to solve.
▶ Write number sentences to go with their answers.

Name _____

Toppling towers

Use 24 small wooden rods to build a tower.
Do it like this:

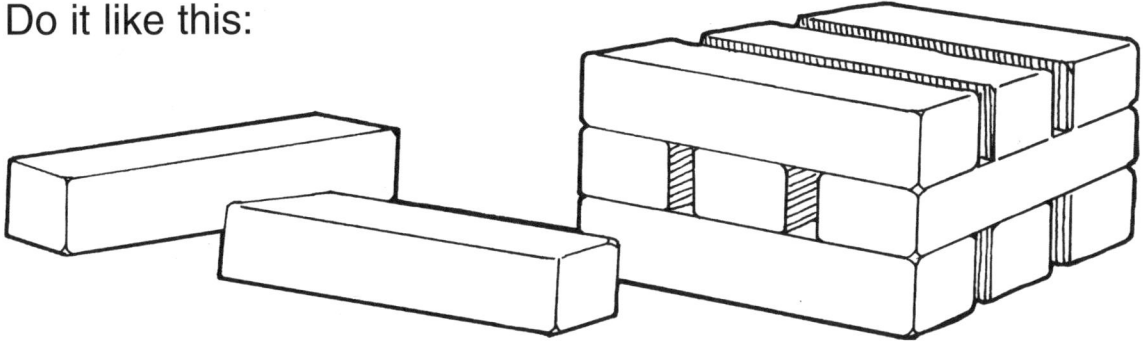

Now take it in turns to pull out one rod – but not from the top.

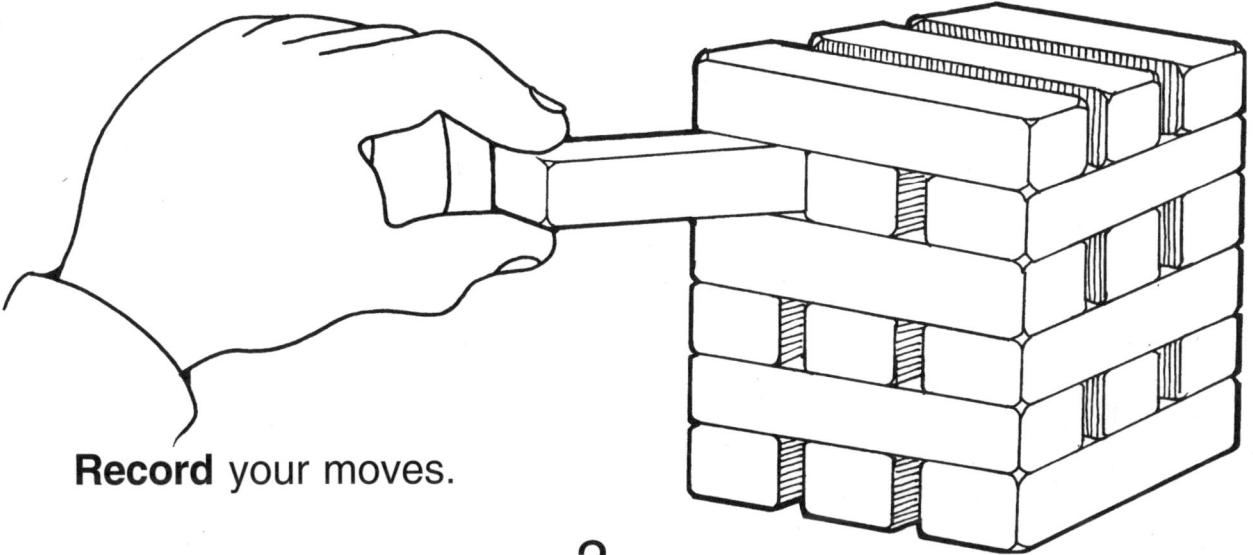

Record your moves.

? ? ?
? ? ?

How many can
you take out
before the tower
falls over?

How many
rods in the
tower just
before it fell?

? ? ?
? ? ?
? ? ?

Only 5 left

Key aims

▶ To explore the relationship between addition and subtraction.
▶ To look for number patterns in subtraction.
▶ To use number statements to describe subtraction.

What you need

▶ 1 activity sheet per child
▶ paper and pencils

The activity

▶ Look at the activity sheet together. Ask the children to suggest how many sweets there could have been to start with.
▶ Take one of their examples and ask them how they could work out how many have been eaten now that there are only five sweets left.
▶ They may suggest:
• using counters;
• drawing the sweets in the bags, and then crossing off the 'eaten' ones.
Offer and explain some of these strategies if the children do not suggest them.
▶ Ask them how to record what they have just done as a number statement.
▶ Explain that they are going to draw a different number of sweets in each bag on their sheet for the number of sweets to start with, and then work out how many sweets have been eaten, when there are only five left. They should record what they've done for each bag as a number statement.
▶ Leave them to complete the activity sheet.

Extension ideas

▶ Record what would happen if the sweets were taken away in twos.
▶ Record examples when two friends both have some of the sweets and work out how many are left at the end.
▶ Use the postermat and write different number stories as to why there are only ten snails left on the wall, for example.

USING & APPLYING

PROBLEM SOLVING
▶ Work systematically.
▶ Select an appropriate method to solve the task.
COMMUNICATION
▶ Talk about what is involved.
▶ Discuss methods with the group.
LOGICAL REASONING
▶ Look for number patterns.

TALK ABOUT

▶ 'If there were eight to start with, how many have been eaten?'
▶ 'How could we work it out?'
▶ 'How could we make a number statement to show what happened?'
▶ 'Can you see a pattern in the numbers you record?'

HERE'S THE MATHS

▶ This activity allows children to use their knowledge of numbers flexibly and to calculate in the way they feel most appropriate. Let them share methods with the group.

WHAT TO LOOK FOR

▶ Does the child work systematically?
▶ Can the child describe his strategies?
▶ Does the child show an intuitive understanding of the relationship between addition and subtraction?
▶ Does the child automatically count on from five sweets?

MORE HELP NEEDED

▶ Encourage children who need help seeing the patterns to reorganise the number statements in a logical order, such as:
$9 - 4 = 5$; $8 - 3 = 5$; $7 - 2 = 5...$

Name _____

I have only 5 sweets left.

How many sweets did I start with?

How many have been eaten?

The biscuit tin

USING & APPLYING

PROBLEM SOLVING
▶ Select the maths to work out the difference.
COMMUNICATION
▶ Use 'more than' and 'less than'.
LOGICAL REASONING
▶ Work out the difference.

TALK ABOUT

▶ 'Which type of biscuit is there most of on this plate?'
▶ 'How many more chocolate biscuits are there than plain ones?'
▶ 'What is the difference?'
▶ 'How many fewer chocolate ones have you got than Jamie?'

HERE'S THE MATHS

▶ Use the terms 'more than' and 'less than' when talking about the biscuits on the plates. The concept of 'difference' is harder to grasp. Referring to it as the extra amount seems to make it easier. Use all of these terms frequently to help the children understand the relationship between them.

WHAT TO LOOK FOR

▶ Does the child have strategies for working out the difference?
▶ Does the child understand the words 'more', 'fewer', 'difference'?
▶ Can the child tell you the difference by 'just knowing'?

MORE HELP NEEDED

▶ The children may need to arrange their biscuits differently so that they can match them, and see the difference.
▶ Children who are having difficulty organising the activity need more practice with simpler activities which involve using real objects.

Key aim

To introduce or clarify the concept of 'difference'.

What you need

▶ card discs in two colours to represent chocolate and plain biscuits – 5 of each per child
▶ a large tin
▶ 1 small paper plate per child
▶ 1 activity sheet per child
▶ paper and pencils

Organisation

▶ Put all the 'biscuits' in the tin, group the children around a table and give out the paper plates.

The activity

▶ The children each take five biscuits from the tin (without looking) and put them on their plates.
▶ Ask who has more plain biscuits on their plate than chocolate ones. Then ask who has more chocolate.
▶ Ask the children to find out how many more chocolate ones they have than plain (or vice versa).
▶ Explain that this extra amount is called the 'difference' between the two.
▶ Give out the activity sheets.
▶ Tell them that they are going to draw plates of chocolate and plain biscuits so that each plate is different. You could get them to show how many of each biscuit each person in the group has; alternatively, let them pick out handfuls each time. Then they need to work out the difference, for each plate.
▶ Leave them to complete the sheet.

Extension ideas

▶ Investigate all the possible combinations of chocolate and plain biscuits (six arrangements are possible with five biscuits on the plate: 5c, 0p; 4c, 1p; 3c, 2p; 2c, 3p; 1c, 4p; 0c, 1p).
▶ Explore plates with a greater number of biscuits in total.

Name _____

The biscuit tin

Difference =

Difference =

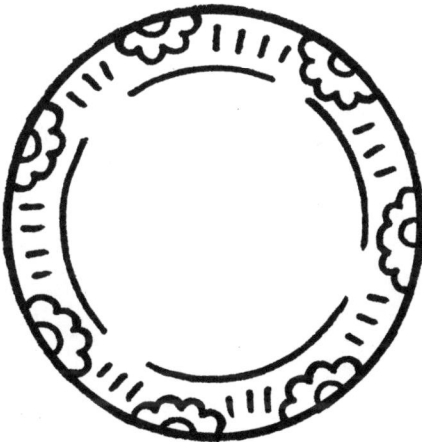

Difference =

Difference =

Difference =

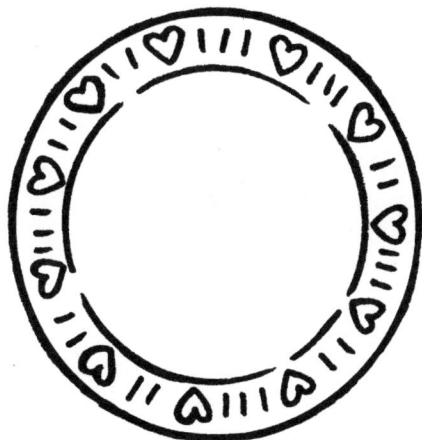

Difference =

USING & APPLYING

PROBLEM SOLVING
▶ Calculate in his or her head.
COMMUNICATION
▶ Explain method of recording.
▶ Explain the rules of the game.
LOGICAL REASONING
▶ Develop a strategy for winning.

TALK ABOUT

▶ *'How did you play?'*
▶ *'How have you recorded it?'*
▶ *'Who took away this 3?'*
▶ *'Does the recording help you to see how to win?'*

HERE'S THE MATHS

▶ This activity involves the children in identifying groups of up to five counters and looking for different combinations possible, especially towards the end. By working out whether they can win or not, they are involved in calculating in their heads and thinking about strategies.

WHAT TO LOOK FOR

▶ Is the child developing strategies for winning?
▶ Can the child explain her strategies, such as 'If I leave 6 she can't win next go'?

MORE HELP NEEDED

▶ Help them to develop a strategy for winning by encouraging them to look at how many counters are left for the other person each time they make a move.
▶ Some children may need more experience of games which involve a simple strategy, such as Noughts and Crosses, to help them to anticipate how to win this game.

Countdown

Key aim
▶ To use subtraction within a game, to develop a strategy for winning.

What you need
▶ 18 counters per pair
▶ paper and pencils
▶ 1 activity sheet per pair

The activity
▶ Go through the activity sheet together.
▶ Have a 'dummy-run' with two people playing, while the rest of the group watches.
▶ It doesn't matter where you take the counters from – so long as they are all from the same row and there are no more than five. The point is that as you reach the end you have to do mental calculations to work out if you can win or not.
▶ Let them play the game in their pairs. Ask them to play it again but this time to record their moves on the back of the activity sheet.
▶ Encourage them to use their recordings to look for any patterns which will give them strategies for winning.
▶ Here is one idea for recording the moves:

Player 1	Player 2	
– 5	– 3	
– 1	– 3	
– 3	– 3	winner

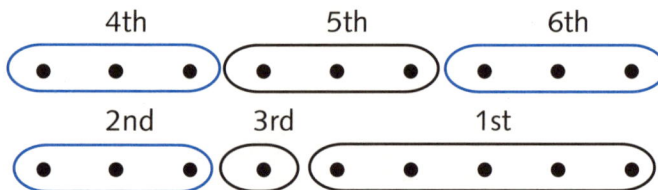

(The two players have different coloured pens).
▶ Leave the children to continue playing and recording.

Extension ideas
▶ Play 'count-up'. Using a calculator, starting from 0, the children take turns to add 1, 2, 3, 4 or 5 to the total. Whoever reaches 18 first is the winner.
▶ Use number sentences to record the games.
▶ Look at the recordings of the moves for each game. Can the children find a way to win always?

Countdown

Here's a game that you win if you're last!

How to play:

- Play with a partner. Line up 18 counters in two equal rows.
- Take turns to take away 1, 2, 3, 4 or 5 counters from *one* row.
- Whoever takes the last group of counters is the winner.

What's next?

USING & APPLYING

COMMUNICATION
▶ Discuss what is involved.
LOGICAL REASONING
▶ Record the patterns.
▶ Predict the next number in the sequence.

TALK ABOUT

▶ 'What number do you think will come next?'
▶ 'How high will the numbers go?'
▶ 'What happens after 0?'
▶ 'What patterns do you notice in your recordings?'

HERE'S THE MATHS

▶ You could provide number lines or number squares to help the children to see the pattern each time.
▶ If they explore what happens below 0 the calculator will take them into negative numbers. How much you explain to them will depend upon their experience, but they need to notice the '−' symbol and be aware that numbers do exist below 0. You could show them a −10 to 10 number line to help them to see what is happening.

WHAT TO LOOK FOR

▶ Can the child predict what number will come next in the sequence?
▶ Can the child explain the pattern and describe what the calculator is doing?

MORE HELP NEEDED

▶ Children who are having difficulty predicting what the calculator will show each time may need more work exploring how a calculator works and exploring on a number line counting on and counting back.

Key aims

▶ To discover number patterns in addition and subtraction.
▶ To encourage prediction, based on existing knowledge of number patterns.
▶ To become aware of negative numbers.

What you need

▶ 1 activity sheet per child
▶ 1 calculator per child
▶ pencils and paper

Organisation

▶ The constant function on most calculators works as shown on the activity sheet. However, check this before you start as some do work differently and you may need to alter the activity sheet accordingly.

The activity

▶ Talk through the activity sheet and let the children all try it on their calculators. Let them tell you what is happening to the numbers.
▶ Ask them to do it again, but this time to record the numbers on their sheet in the given space. Encourage them to guess what the next number will be before they press the '=' key.
▶ Let them explore using the calculator in this way with different start numbers (the first number box). They can then explore with different addition numbers and then with different subtraction numbers (the second number box in each case). Encourage them to record what they find.

Extension ideas

▶ Record the number patterns on number squares.
▶ Use the number lines on page 47 (including −10 to −1) to record the numbers explored in each sequence.
▶ Invent their own game using the constant function.

Name _____

What's next?

Press [ON/C]

[1] [+] [+] [1] [=] [=]

Keep pressing [=]

What happens?

Do it again.

Guess what the number will be before you press [=]

Write the numbers here:

Now try [ON/C] [1] [0] [–] [–] [1] [=] [=]

Guess what the number will be before you press [=]

What happens?

Write the numbers here:

Try it again with some other numbers.

Number and operation cards

0	1	2	3
4	5	6	7
8	9	10	+
−	=	+	−

FEWER OR GREATER?
MATHS FOCUS – NUMBER KIT 1

PHOTOCOPIABLE

Number line

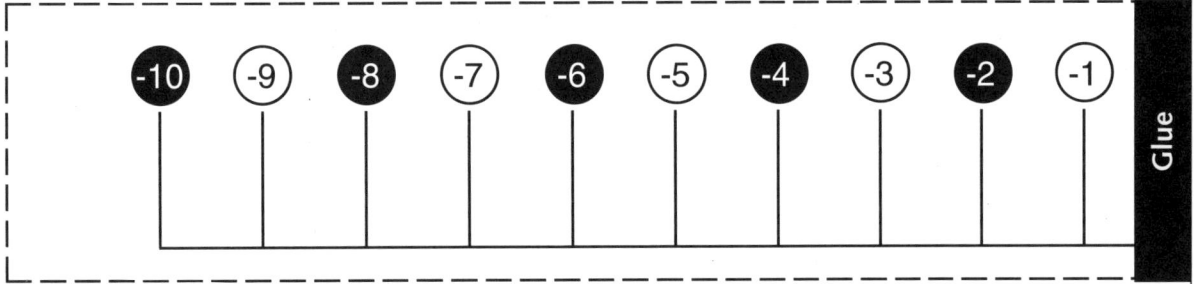

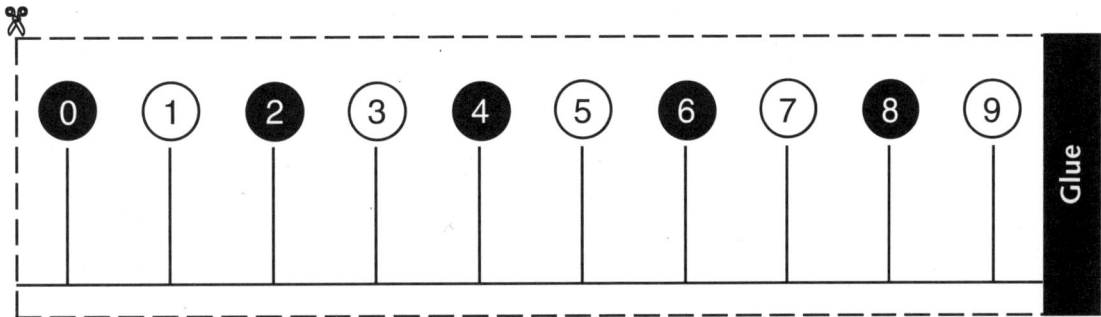

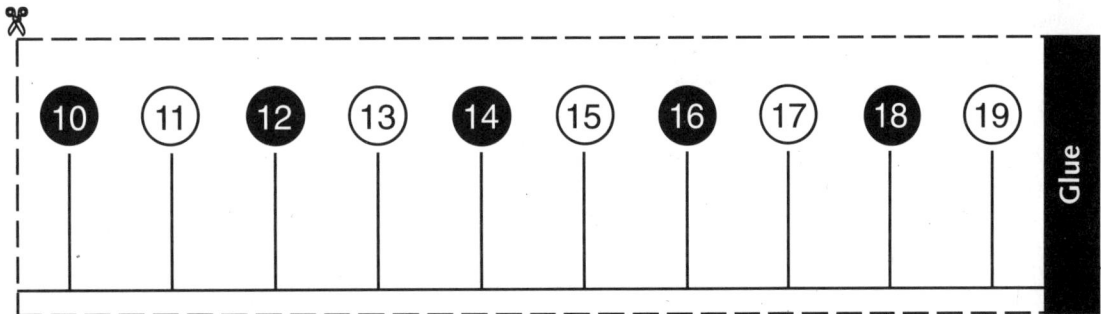

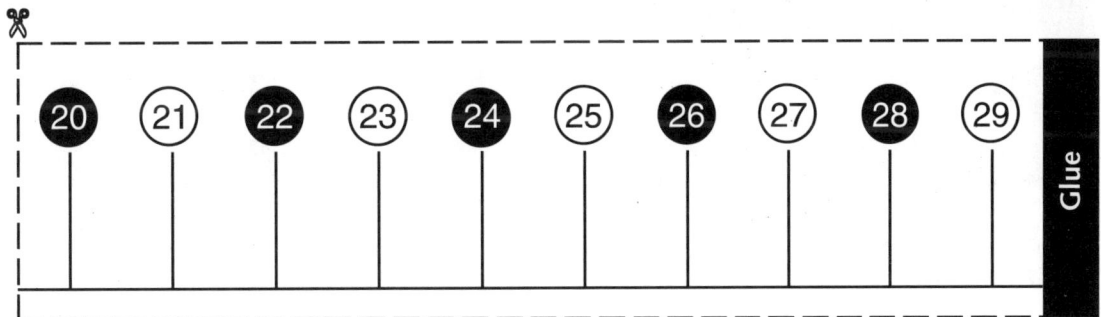

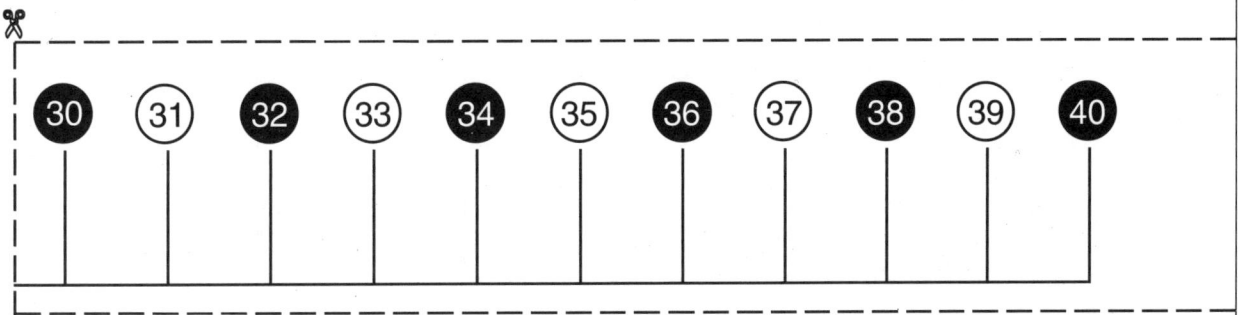

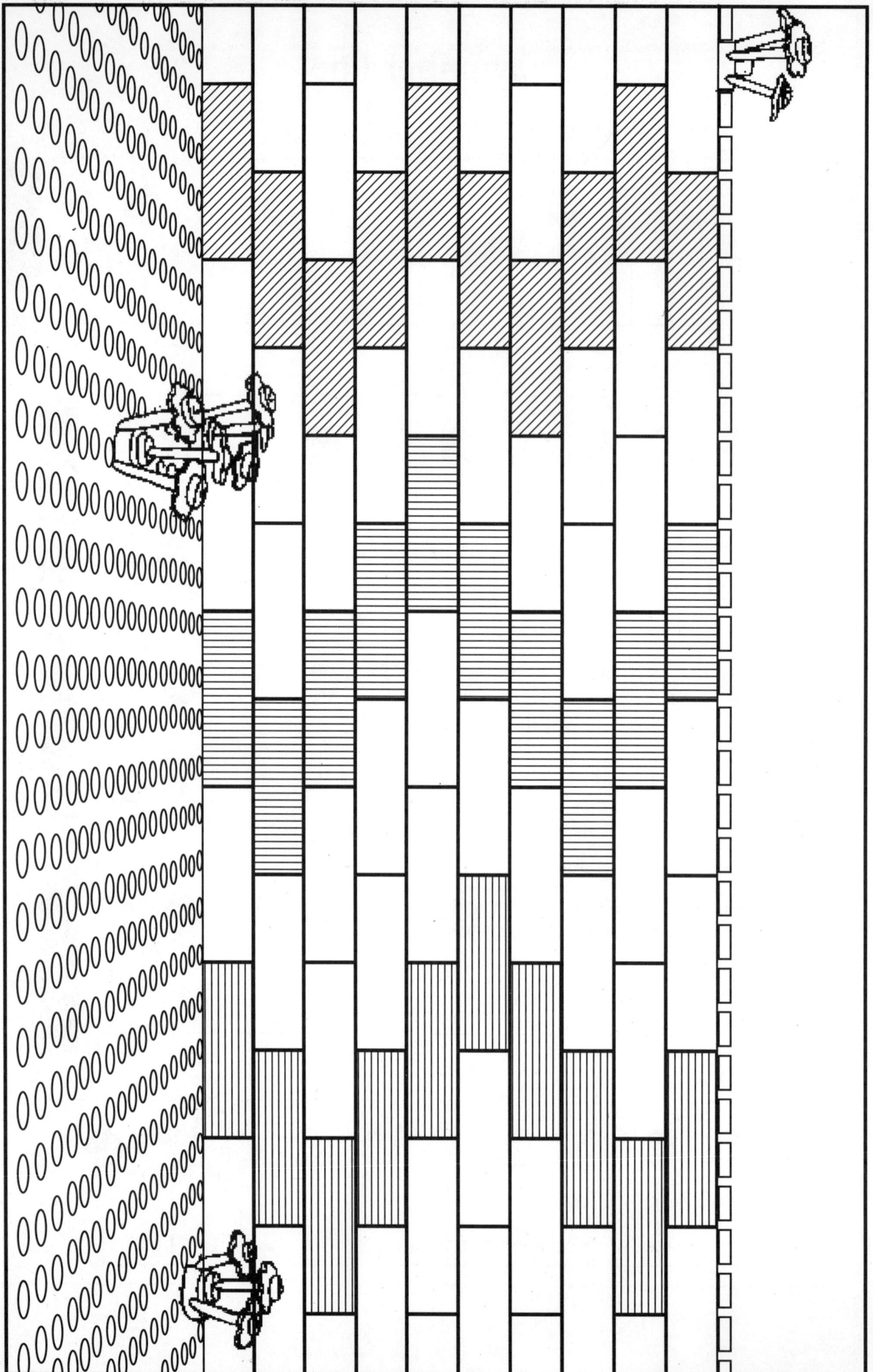

FEWER OR GREATER?
MATHS FOCUS – NUMBER KIT 1

PHOTOCOPIABLE